Ben Roethlisberger

by Michael Sandler

Consultant: Norries Wilson
Head Football Coach, Columbia University

BEARPORT
PUBLISHING

New York, New York

Credits

Cover, © zsports/NewsCom; Title Page, © Andy Lyons/Getty Images; 4, © Jason Arnold/
Reuters/Landov; 5, © AP Images/Luis M. Alvarez; 6, © Scott Boehm/Getty Images; 7, © Andy
Lyons/Getty Images; 8L, Courtesy of Jerry Snodgrass; 8R, Courtesy of Jerry Snodgrass; 9, ©
Michael J. LeBrecht II/Sports Illustrated/Getty Images; 10, © Brett Hansbauer; 11, © Chris
Trotman/Getty Images; 12, © Archie Carpenter/UPI Photo/Landov; 13, © Rick Stewart/Getty
Images; 14, © Steve C. Michell/epa/Corbis; 15, © Marc Serota/Reuters/Corbis; 16, Courtesy
Bigbennews.com; 17, Courtesy Bigbennews.com; 18, © Pittsburgh Post-Gazette; 19, © Scott
Dietz/412foto.com; 20, © AP Images/Keith B. Srakocic; 21, © AP Images/The Courier/Howard
Moyer; 22, © Andy Lyons/Getty Images; 22Logo, © KRT/Newscom.

Publisher: Kenn Goin
Senior Editor: Lisa Wiseman
Creative Director: Spencer Brinker
Photo Researcher: Omni-Photo Communications, Inc.
Design: Dawn Beard Creative

Library of Congress Cataloging-in-Publication Data

Sandler, Michael, 1965–
  Ben Roethlisberger / by Michael Sandler.
      p. cm. — (Football heroes making a difference)
  Includes bibliographical references and index.
  ISBN-13: 978-1-59716-770-3 (library binding)
  ISBN-10: 1-59716-770-3 (library binding)
  1. Roethlisberger, Ben, 1982—Juvenile literature. 2. Football players—United States—
Biography—Juvenile literature. I. Title.

  GV939.R64S36 2009
  796.33092—dc22
  [B]
                                    2008042446

For more information, write to Bearport Publishing Company, Inc., 101 Fifth Avenue, Suite 6R,
New York, New York 10003. Printed in the United States of America.

10 9 8 7 6 5 4 3 2 1

CONTENTS

Suddenly a Starter

This was Ben Roethlisberger's big test. For the very first time, the young Pittsburgh Steeler was **starting** at quarterback.

Pittsburgh had planned to go slow with the rookie. He wasn't supposed to play much at first. Now plans had changed. Pittsburgh's top two quarterbacks were hurt. Only Ben was left to face the Miami Dolphins. Could he handle the job?

On the game's first play, Ben dropped back to pass. Miami **defenders** were all over the Steelers' **receivers**. Ben let the ball fly anyway— right into the hands of Miami **cornerback** Patrick Surtain. **Interception**! "Not good," Ben thought.

Ben throws the ball during the game against the Dolphins.

Ben's first NFL start was on September 26, 2004, the third week of the season.

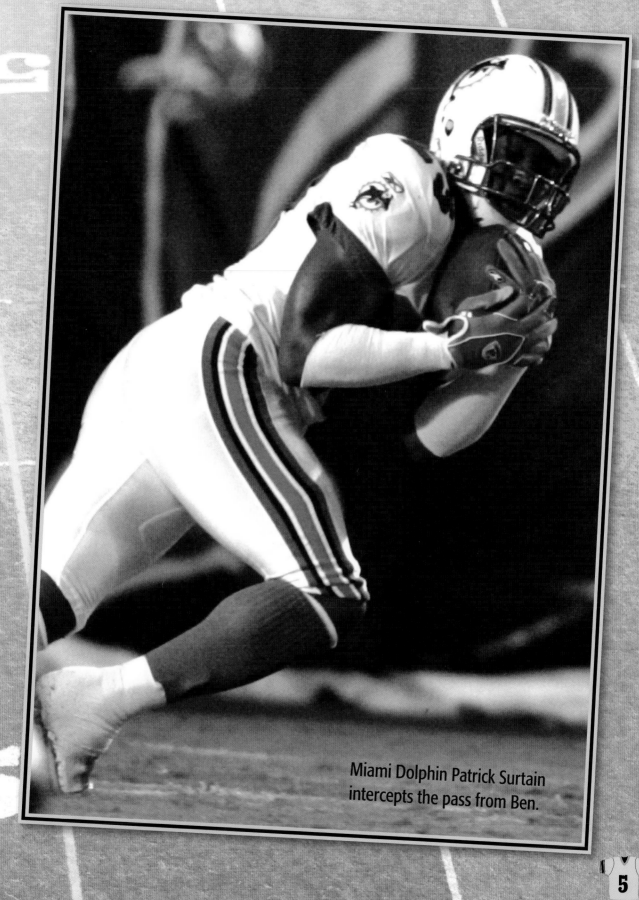

Miami Dolphin Patrick Surtain intercepts the pass from Ben.

Amazing

Most rookies would have crumbled after beginning a game with a **turnover**. Ben didn't. He stayed calm and cool, and waited for another chance.

On the next **possession**, Ben threw a 42-yard (38-m) pass to set up a Pittsburgh field goal. The Steelers took the lead and never gave it up. The rookie had his first win.

A week later, in a game against the Cincinnati Bengals, Ben got his second win. Then, the following Sunday, Pittsburgh beat the Cleveland Browns. With Ben at quarterback, the Steelers couldn't lose. By season's end, he had won 13 straight games.

Ben celebrates a touchdown during the game against the Cleveland Browns in 2004.

One of the 13 games won in 2004 was against the New England Patriots. Ben completed 18 out of 24 passes without an interception.

Ben's 13-game winning streak was the longest for a rookie in the history of the NFL.

Growing Up

Growing up in Findlay, Ohio, Ben never thought about NFL wins. As a kid, he dreamed of becoming a secret agent. He spent hours climbing up and down the tree in front of his house—pretending to be on missions. He also practiced daredevil stunts on a trampoline.

In fact, football wasn't even his favorite sport. Basketball was. Ben spent hours working on his **jumper**.

Still, Ben's sturdy body and exceptional strength made him a natural for football. At Findlay High School, he became a star in football, basketball, and baseball, too!

Ben playing basketball in high school

Ben (#7) played quarterback for the Findlay High School Trojans.

Ben and his family

Ben had a busy senior year of high school. He hit .300 as the baseball team's shortstop, averaged 26.5 points per game as the basketball team's **point guard**, and threw 54 touchdown passes as the football team's quarterback.

Choosing Football

After high school, Ben headed to Miami University in Ohio. By now football was his number-one sport. He was a very good basketball player, but he was a spectacular quarterback.

Ben's throwing arm was both powerful and **accurate**. In three seasons playing for the RedHawks at Miami, he broke almost every school passing record. He was also a winner. In his final season, he led his small school to a **top ten ranking**.

Ben was **drafted** out of college by the Pittsburgh Steelers. Pittsburgh saw him as their quarterback of the future.

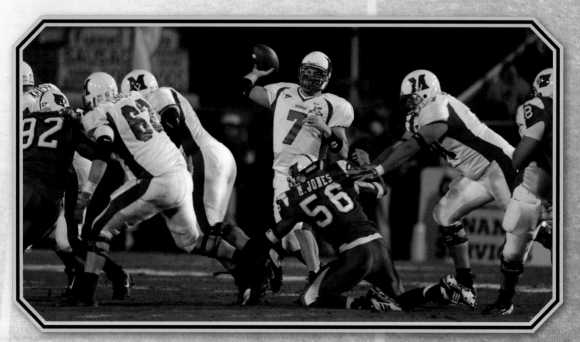

Ben helped the RedHawks win the GMAC Bowl with a 49-28 victory over Louisville.

Pittsburgh picked Ben in the first round of the 2004 NFL draft.

During his college years, the university's basketball coaches kept asking Ben to play hoops, too. Ben turned them down, however. He wanted to **dedicate** all his time to football.

Surprising the Steelers

Steelers fans were excited to have Ben on their team. They were even more thrilled when he stepped in and won 13 straight games.

Surprisingly, Ben stayed **humble** despite this success. He felt that his teammates were just as important to the Steelers' success as he was. Everyone had made a difference—especially receivers such as Hines Ward and running back Jerome Bettis.

There was another reason why Ben wasn't **smug**. His dream rookie season ended short of the Super Bowl. Unfortunately, the New England Patriots beat Pittsburgh in the **AFC Championship Game**.

Hines Ward (#86) takes a pass from Ben and gains 15 yards (14 m) during a win against the Washington Redskins in 2004.

Ben (#7) hands off the ball
to Jerome Bettis (#36).

Ben was named NFL **Offensive** Rookie
of the Year after the 2004 season.

Super Bowl Success

The Pittsburgh Steelers had won four Super Bowls. Ben admired the trophies that were locked in the team's office. He wouldn't be happy until he helped Pittsburgh get another one.

In 2005, Ben got the chance. Pittsburgh made the playoffs for the second straight year. Then they beat the Indianapolis Colts and the Denver Broncos to reach football's biggest game.

Ben overcame a rough start to make some key plays for his team during Super Bowl XL (40). The Steelers beat the Seattle Seahawks, 21-10. In just his second season, Ben had **achieved** his goal.

Quarterbacks rarely make tackles, but Ben (#7) was able to stop the Colts' Nick Harper (#25) to save a playoff win for Pittsburgh.

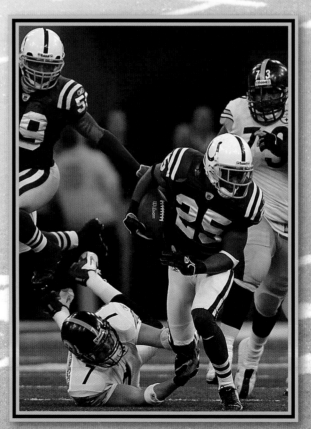

Winning a Super Bowl, said Ben (center), "is one of the best feelings you can ever experience."

At age 23, Ben was the youngest quarterback ever to win a Super Bowl.

Service to Others

Though winning the Super Bowl was amazing, Ben knows some things are even more important—like helping others and changing people's lives. For this reason, he started the Ben Roethlisberger **Foundation** in 2006.

One of its biggest goals is to help police and fire departments buy **service dogs**. These specially trained dogs sniff out bombs, find hidden drugs, and help track down missing people.

Who got the first dog? Ben's hometown did—the Findlay, Ohio, Police Department. "I received a call that someone wanted to buy us a new dog. I knew it was Ben," said Findlay Police Chief Bill Spraw.

Ben and one of his dogs

Ben and some police
officers with a service dog
that he donated to their
department

Ben's foundation tries to buy a service dog for
police or fire departments in every town where
the Steelers play. In 2007, this included Cleveland,
Ohio; Phoenix, Arizona; and New York City.

Working with Kids

Helping children is also important to Ben. In Findlay, Ben sponsors a youth football program, which gives kids a chance to learn the game. He is trying to build the town a new youth football **complex**, too.

Ben also helps kids who live in Pittsburgh, Pennsylvania. He spends time visiting schools in the city. At middle schools and high schools, he gives kids advice about making good choices, staying away from drugs, and doing their best. At grade schools, he speaks with kids about how important it is to learn how to read.

Ben visits a grade school in Pittsburgh.

At the annual Ben Roethlisberger Football Camp, Ben teaches kids skills and raises money for his foundation.

Ben has his own barbecue sauce called Big Ben's BBQ. It comes in mild, spicy, and hot. Money from each type sold goes to **charity**.

Bouncing Back

In 2006, things got tough for Ben. First, he had a serious motorcycle accident. He recovered from his injuries, but that year, Pittsburgh missed the playoffs.

After the season, Ben thought back to his first NFL start. He remembered how he had bounced back after his interception. He knew he could do it again.

In 2007, Ben did just that. He had his best season as a passer and guided the Steelers back into the playoffs. Ben had made a difference once more.

Ben (#7) breaks a tackle during a playoff game after the 2007 season.

Ben spends time with some of his young fans.

After the 2007 season, Ben was named to his first **Pro Bowl**.

The Ben File

Ben is a football hero on and off the field. Here are some highlights.

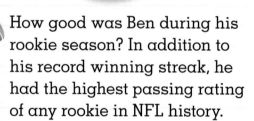

- How good was Ben during his rookie season? In addition to his record winning streak, he had the highest passing rating of any rookie in NFL history.

- Why does Ben's foundation focus on dogs? Ben loves the animals. When he was a kid, there were always dogs around his house. He is now the proud owner of two!

- Ben throws long passes. He averages over 8 yards (7 m) on each throw. That's the fourth highest average in league history.

- Ben's nickname "Big Ben" doesn't refer to his size. It comes from a game-winning pass Ben made in college that was called a "Big Ben." After he made the pass, the play's name became his nickname.

- Some police departments already have dogs. So Ben buys them service dog equipment, such as bulletproof dog vests, instead.

Glossary

accurate (AK-yuh-ruht) precise, on target

achieved (uh-CHEEVD) completed, reached

AFC Championship Game (AY-EFF-SEE CHAM-pee-uhn-*ship* GAME) a playoff game that decides which AFC (American Football Conference) team will go to the Super Bowl

charity (CHA-ruh-tee) groups that try to help people in need

complex (KOM-pleks) a group of buildings used for a specific purpose

cornerback (KOR-nur-bak) a player on defense who usually covers the other team's receivers

dedicate (DED-uh-kayt) to put a lot of time and energy into something

defenders (di-FEN-durz) players who have the job of trying to stop the other team from scoring

drafted (DRAFT-id) picked after college to play for an NFL team

foundation (foun-DAY-shuhn) an organization that supports or gives money to worthwhile causes

humble (HUHM-buhl) modest, not overly proud

interception (*in*-tur-SEP-shuhn) a pass that is caught by a player on the defensive team

jumper (JUHMP-ur) a basketball shot in which a player jumps first and then shoots the ball

offensive (aw-FEN-siv) a kind of player whose job is to score points

point guard (POINT GARD) the basketball player who controls the ball and sets up plays for his or her teammates

possession (puh-ZESH-uhn) when a team has the ball and is trying to score

Pro Bowl (PROH BOHL) the yearly all-star game for the season's best NFL players

receivers (ri-SEE-vurz) players whose job it is to catch passes

service dogs (SUR-viss DAWGS) dogs that are trained for specific jobs

smug (SMUHG) very pleased with oneself

starting (START-ing) playing at the beginning of a game

top ten ranking (TOP TEN RANK-ing) a list of the ten best college football teams in the country

turnover (TURN-oh-vur) a play that results in the loss of the football to the other team

Bibliography

Farmer, Sam. "The Man with the Golden Arm." *Los Angeles Times* (November 28, 2004).

Robinson, Alan. "Football Not Roethlisberger's First Love." *AP Sports* (February 4, 2006).

Silver, Michael. "Ben There, Done That." *Sports Illustrated* (November 8, 2004).

Read More

Sandler, Michael. *Hines Ward and the Pittsburgh Steelers: Super Bowl XL.* New York: Bearport (2007).

Schmalzbauer, Adam. *The History of the Pittsburgh Steelers.* Mankato, MN: Creative Education (2005).

Zuehlke, Jeffrey. *Ben Roethlisberger.* Minneapolis, MN: Lerner (2007).

Learn More Online

To learn more about Ben Roethlisberger,
the Ben Roethlisberger Foundation, and the Pittsburgh Steelers, visit
www.bearportpublishing.com/FootballHeroes

Index